Cursive Handwriting Practice for Kids

Children's Reading & Writing Education Books

Speedy Publishing LLC
40 E. Main St. #1156
Newark, DE 19711
www.speedypublishing.com

Cursive  Handwriting

A A A A A

A A A A A

B B B B B

B B B B B

Cursive Handwriting

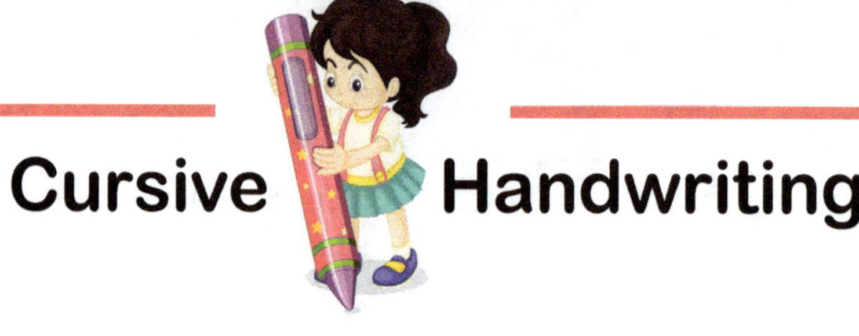

C C C C C

C C C C C

D D D D D

D D D D D

Cursive Handwriting

E E E E E

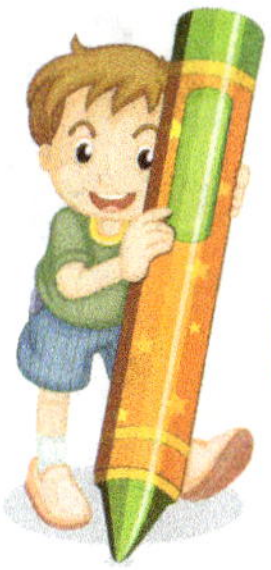

E E E E E

F F F F F

F F F F F

Cursive Handwriting

G G G G G

G G G G G

H H H H H

H H H H H

Cursive Handwriting

I I I I I

I I I I I

J J J J J

J J J J J

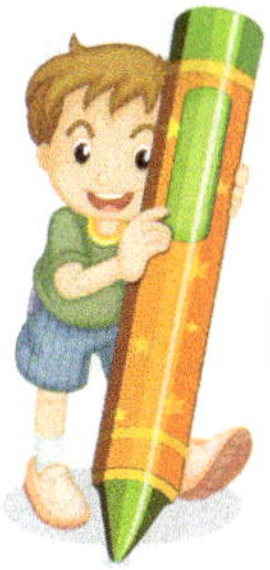

K K K K K

K K K K K

L L L L L

L L L L L

Cursive Handwriting

Cursive Handwriting

O O O O O

O O O O O

p p p p p

p p p p p

Cursive  Handwriting

Q Q Q Q Q

Q Q Q Q Q

R R R R R

R R R R R

Cursive Handwriting

S S S S S

S S S S S

T T T T T

T T T T T

U U U U U

U U U U U

V V V V V

V V V V V

w w w w w

w w w w w

x x x x x

x x x x x

Cursive  Handwriting

y y y y y

y y y y y

z z z z z

z z z z z

Cursive Handwriting

a a a a a

a a a a a

b b b b b

b b b b b

Cursive Handwriting

c c c c c

c c c c c

d d d d d

d d d d d

Cursive Handwriting

e e e e e

e e e e e

f f f f f

f f f f f

Cursive Handwriting

g g g g g

g g g g g

h h h h h

h h h h h

Cursive Handwriting

i i i i i

i i i i i

j j j j j

j j j j j

k *k* *k* *k* *k*

k *k* *k* *k* *k*

l *l* *l* *l* *l*

l *l* *l* *l* *l*

Cursive Handwriting

m m m m m

m m m m m

n n n n n

n n n n n

Cursive Handwriting

q q q q q

q q q q q

r r r r r

r r r r r

Cursive Handwriting

i i i i i

i i i i i

t t t t t

t t t t t

Cursive Handwriting

U *U* *U* *U* *U*

U *U* *U* *U* *U*

u *u* *u* *u* *u*

u *u* *u* *u* *u*

w w w w w

w w w w w

x x x x x

x x x x x

Cursive Handwriting

y y y y y

y y y y y

z z z z z

z z z z z

Cursive  Handwriting

Your complete name in cursive handwriting:

Your father's name in cursive handwriting:

Cursive  Handwriting

Your mother's name in cursive handwriting:

Your address in cursive handwriting:

Cursive Handwriting

Your favorite teacher in cursive handwriting:

Your school name in cursive handwriting:

Cursive Handwriting

Your favorite TV show in cursive handwriting:

Your favorite cartoon character in cursive handwriting:

Cursive Handwriting

Your favorite hobby in cursive handwriting:

Your favorite quote in cursive handwriting:

Cursive  Handwriting

Your favorite book in cursive handwriting:

Your bestfriend's name in cursive handwriting:

Cursive  Handwriting

Your favorite song in cursive handwriting:

Your favorite singer in cursive handwriting:

Cursive Handwriting

Your favorite food in cursive handwriting:

Your favorite sport in cursive handwriting:

Cursive Handwriting

Your favorite movie in cursive handwriting:

Your favorite superhero in cursive handwriting:

Cursive Handwriting

Your goal/s in cursive handwriting:

Your ambition in cursive handwriting:

Cursive  Handwriting

Your favorite brand in cursive handwriting:

Your favorite subject in cursive handwriting:

www.ingramcontent.com/pod-product-compliance
Lightning Source LLC
LaVergne TN
LVHW060832170826
845678LV00010B/1962